Recorder Wizard

Follow the **magical** comic strip adventures of Johnny and Sophie as the Recorder Wizard teaches you how to play!

By Emma Coulthard

T0087660

Contents

Published by
Chester Music
8/9 Frith Street, London W1D 3JB, England.

Exclusive Distributors:
Music Sales Corporation
257 Park Avenue South,
New York, NY10010,
United States of America.
Music Sales Limited
Distribution Centre,
Newmarket Road,
Bury St Edmunds,
Suffolk IP33 3YB, England.
Music Sales Pty Limited
120 Rothschild Avenue,
Rosebery, NSW 2018,
Australia.

Order No. CH68575
ISBN 0-8256-3338-9
This book © Copyright 2004 by Chester Music.

Unauthorized reproduction of any part of this publication by any means including photocopying is an infringement of copyright.

Written by Emma Coulthard
Project editor Heather Ramage
Illustrated by Bob Bond
Comic strip plot by Ed Chatelier
Art agency The Edge Group
Design and layout Chloë Alexander Design
Music setting Michael McCartney

CD recorded, mixed, and mastered by Jonas Persson
Music arranged by Rick Cardinali
Recorder Emma Coulthard
Voice-over artist Mike Winsor

Your Guarantee of Quality:
As publishers, we strive to produce every book to the highest commercial standards.
The music has been freshly engraved and the book has been carefully designed to minimize awkward page turns and to make playing from it a real pleasure.
Throughout, the printing and binding have been planned to ensure a sturdy, attractive publication which should give years of enjoyment.
If your copy fails to meet our high standards, please inform us and we will gladly replace it.

www.recorderwizard.com

The Three Skills

1 The Breath of a Soft Breeze

Breathe deeply and
blow gently at your hand.

Feel the cool air
on your fingers.

2 The Power of Speech

You must speak into the recorder
to make a nice, clear sound.

DOO...DOO...
DOO...DOO...

Practice saying
doo, doo, doo, doo...

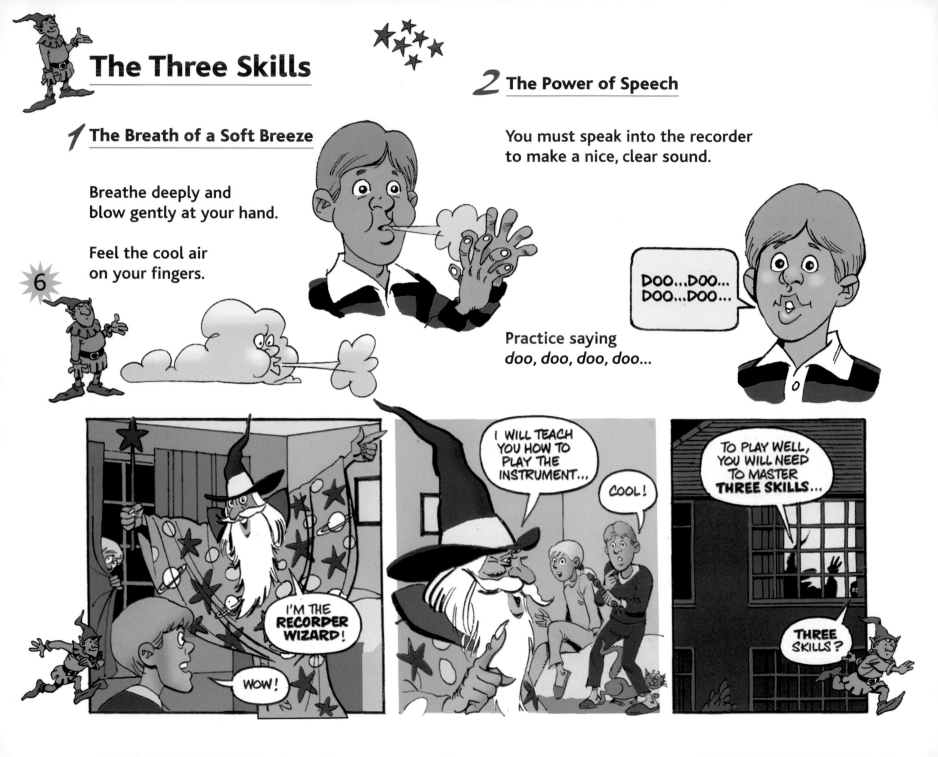

3 Dancing Fingers

Place your fingers on the holes.

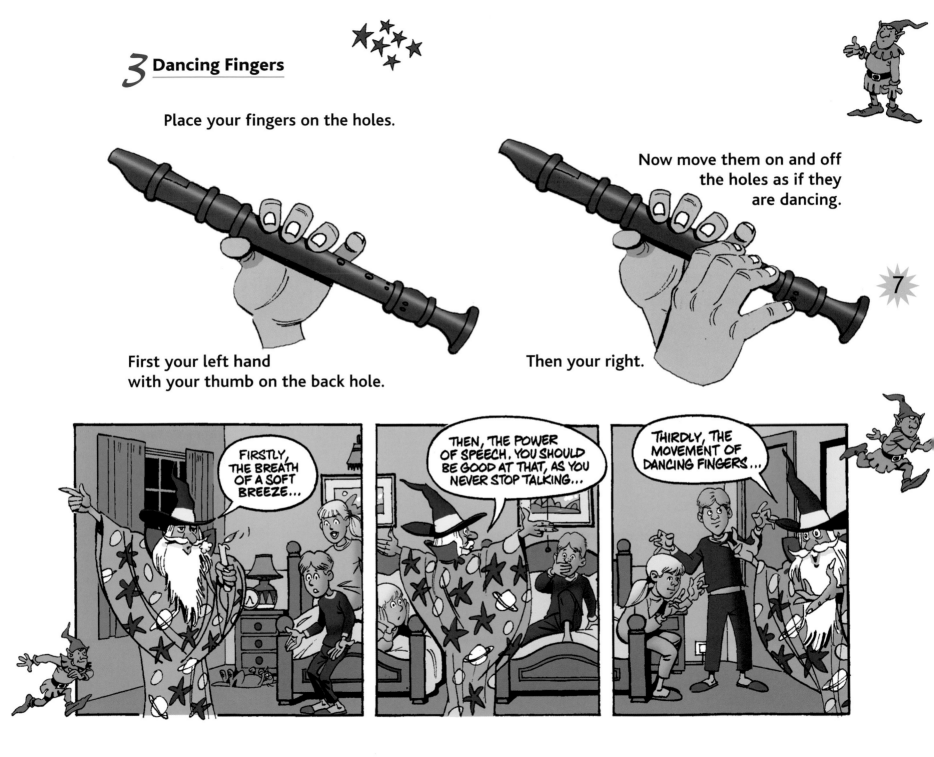

First your left hand
with your thumb on the back hole.

Now move them on and off
the holes as if they
are dancing.

Then your right.

B Is for Broomstick

This is how you play B

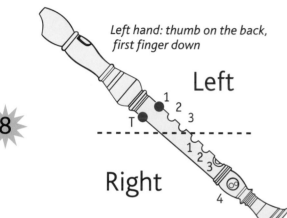

Left hand: thumb on the back, first finger down

Left

T 1 2 3

Right

1 2 3

4

Try some long Bs:

B —————— B ——————

B —————— B ——————

And some short ones:

B — B — B — B —

Remember to blow gently, and to say *doo*!

Magic B

This is the staff.

This is called a treble clef.
It sits at the beginning of each staff.

B, B, ma - gic B, try to cast a spell on me!

The staff has five lines and four spaces, and B is written on the middle line.

9

A Is for Apple

Here is A

Left hand: thumb on the back, first two fingers down

Left

Right

Try some long ones:

A ——— A ———

A ——— A ———

And some short ones:

A— A— A— A—

Say *doo* with your tongue and speak each note clearly.

How many things beginning with 'A' can you find in the comic strip above?

A A hip - hoo - ray!

Here's an - oth - er note to play.

A is written on the second space up.

11

Dance with Me

So - phie, dance with me

12

un - der - neath the ap - ple tree

Repeat!

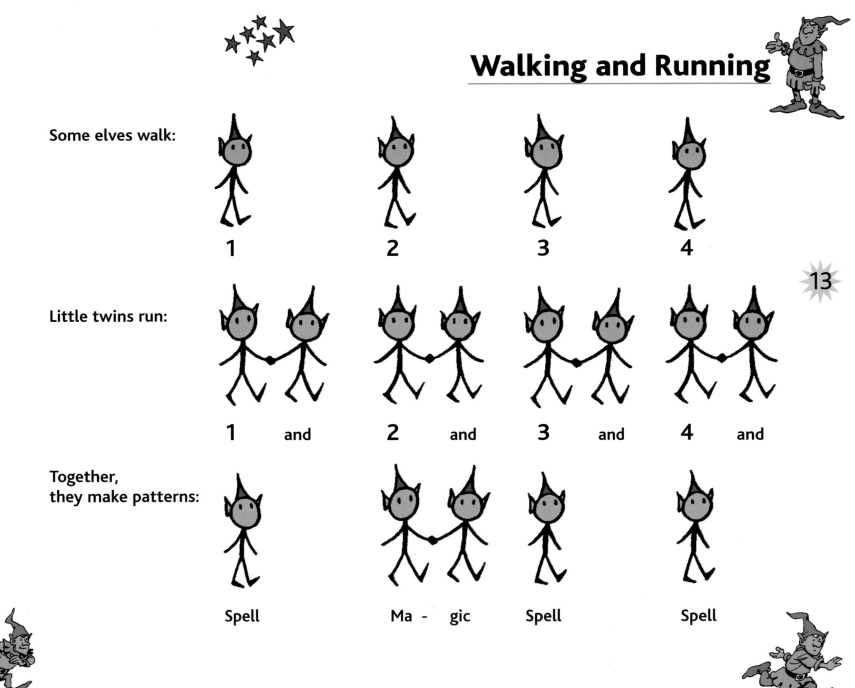

Some elves walk:

1   2   3   4

Little twins run:

1   and   2   and   3   and   4   and

Together,
they make patterns:

Spell   Ma - gic   Spell   Spell

13

G Is for Ghost

This is G

Left hand: thumb on the back, three fingers down

Left

Right

G is written on the second line up.

Speak each note gently.

G, G, Ghost ... ooooh!

G, G, Ghost ... ooooh!

15

How many things beginning with 'G' can you find in the comic strip above?

Have a Rest

When an elf needs to rest, he has a little sleep.

When we want silence in music, we have a little rest:

There are long rests and short rests.

16

This one lasts for just one beat – so don't fall asleep!

Three Blind Mice

The vertical lines are called barlines.

They divide the notes into groups of equal length, called bars.

The number at the beginning of the music tells you how many beats are in each bar.

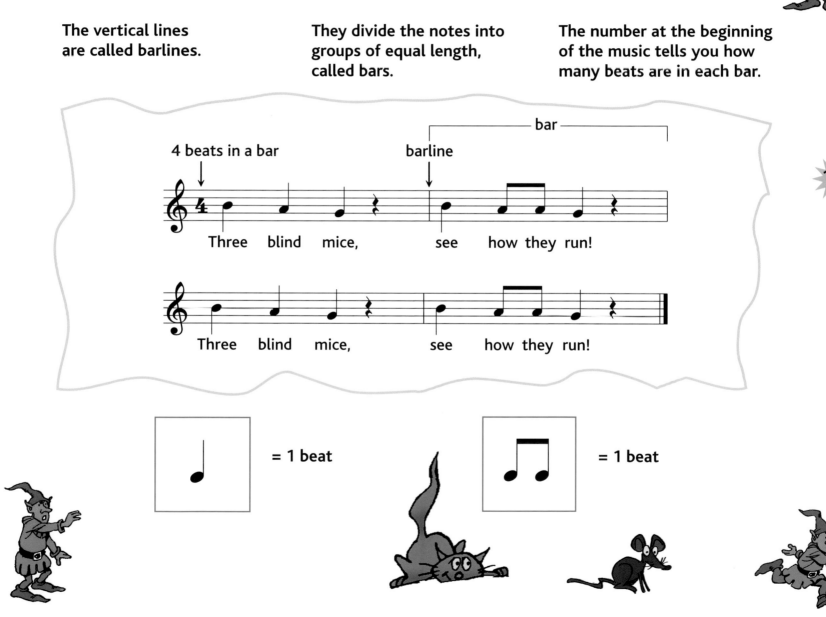

4 beats in a bar

barline

bar

Three blind mice, see how they run!

Three blind mice, see how they run!

17

= 1 beat

= 1 beat

Mary Had a Little Lamb

This piece has four beats in a bar.
Play slowly, one beat at a time, until you are ready to put it all together.

19

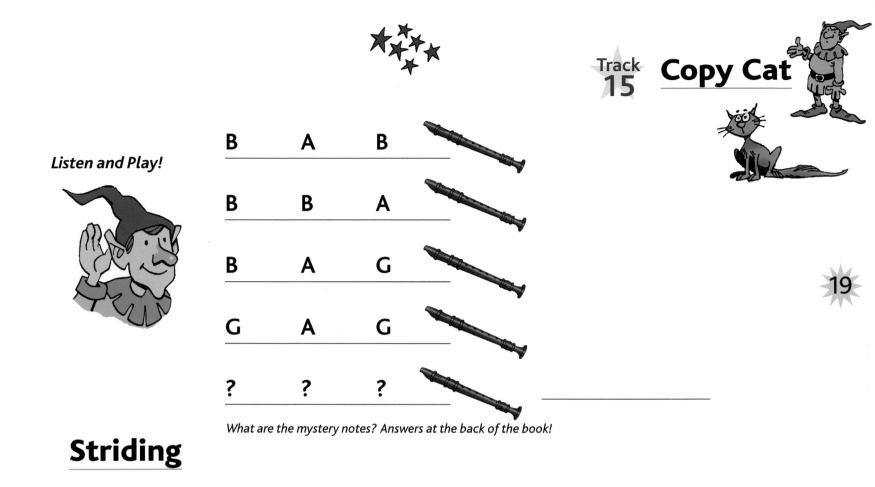

Listen and Play!

B	A	B
B	B	A
B	A	G
G	A	G
?	?	?

What are the mystery notes? Answers at the back of the book!

Striding

Apart from walking and running, some elves like to take big strides.

In music, it looks like this:

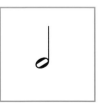

The stride takes up two beats: 1   2   **(two beats)**

E Is for Enchanted

This is E

Left hand: thumb on the back, three fingers down

Left

Right

Right hand: first two fingers down

20

E is written on the bottom line.

Speak in a whisper!

3 beats in a bar

En - chant - ed E, What can you see?

Look right a - bove you I'm up in a tree.

21

Forest Sounds

You can make amazing sound effects on the recorder.

Owls

22

E is good for owls.

Too - whit,   too - woo!

Yellow Bird

This ⌣ or ⌢ is a *slur*. It tells you to join the notes together without tonguing in between.

Just speak the first note and move your fingers for the others in the slur.

Yel - low bird,
doo _____

yel - low bird.
doo _____

Cuckoos

B and G sounds like a cuckoo. The dot on the note tells you to make the sound really short. It's called a *staccato*. Say *tut* with your tongue, instead of *doo*.

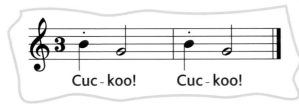

Cuc - koo!   Cuc - koo!

Murmuring Stream

Slurring repeated notes together makes a lovely murmuring sound.

doo _____   *doo* _____

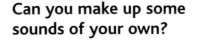

Can you make up some sounds of your own?

Song of the Elves

*T*he elves perform a magic dance,
  and when they stop, they clap their hands.

. . . .

*T*hey leap about and shout and scream,
  with lots of clapping in between.

. . . .

24

*T*he order of the cards is clear,
  but which is which? Just use your ear!

. . . .

*A*nd if you are in any doubt,
  you're going to have to work it out!

. . . .

Rhythm Puzzle

Clapping is a hoot!

These are the clapping rhythms from the song,
but they are in the wrong order.

Can you work out which is which
by listening to the song,
and then write them in the boxes?

Answers at the back of the book!

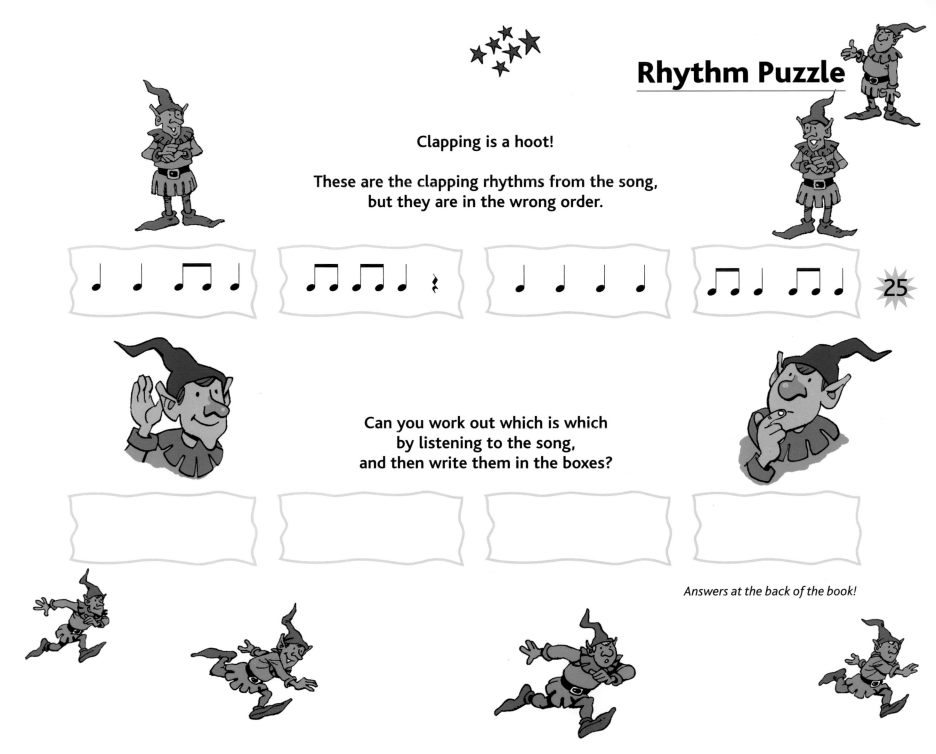

D Is for Dragon

Tracks 24-25

26

Make sure all the holes are covered or you'll get a nasty squeak!

Left hand: thumb on the back, three fingers down

Left

Right

Right hand: three fingers down

D is written underneath the staff.

Say *doo* quietly – don't wake the dragon!

Very gently

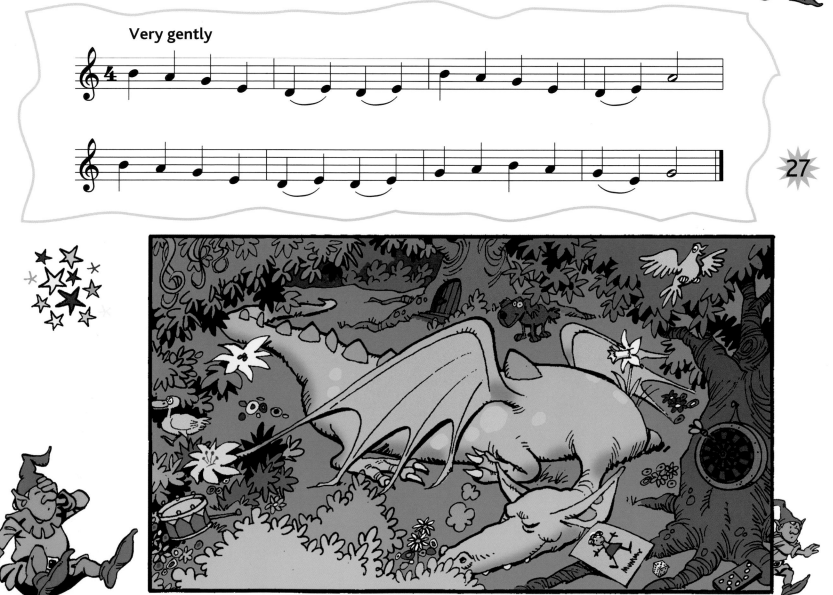

27

How many things beginning with 'D' can you find in the picture above?

The Dragon's Lair

29

Lullaby

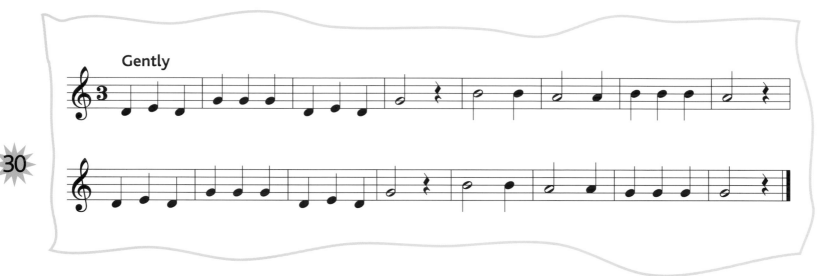

30

Secret Words Puzzle

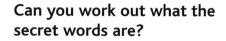

Can you work out what the
secret words are?

Write the letter names
underneath the notes.

Answers at the back of the book!

March to the Castle

Tracks 34-35

Welcome to my home!

Write down each note letter to find out the password - then speak for access.

Oh, and please wipe your feet!

Thank you,

Wizard

--- --- --- --- --- --- ---

Answer at the back of the book!

33

Clock Chimes

This note: lasts for three beats.

You'll need plenty of air!

Trumpet Fanfare

Brightly

35

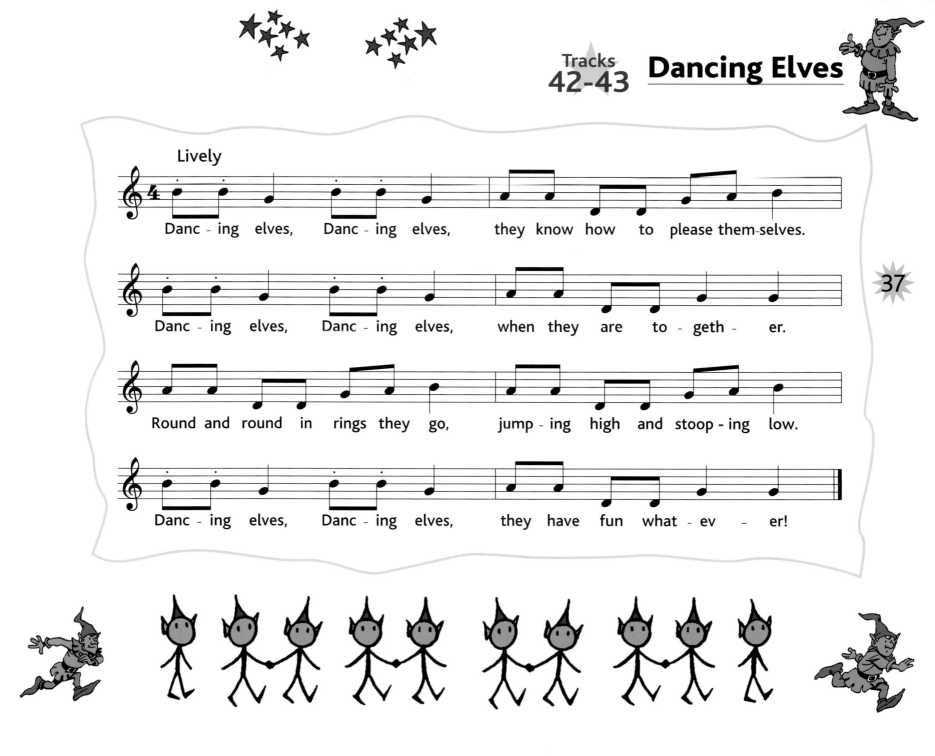

Uncle Angus

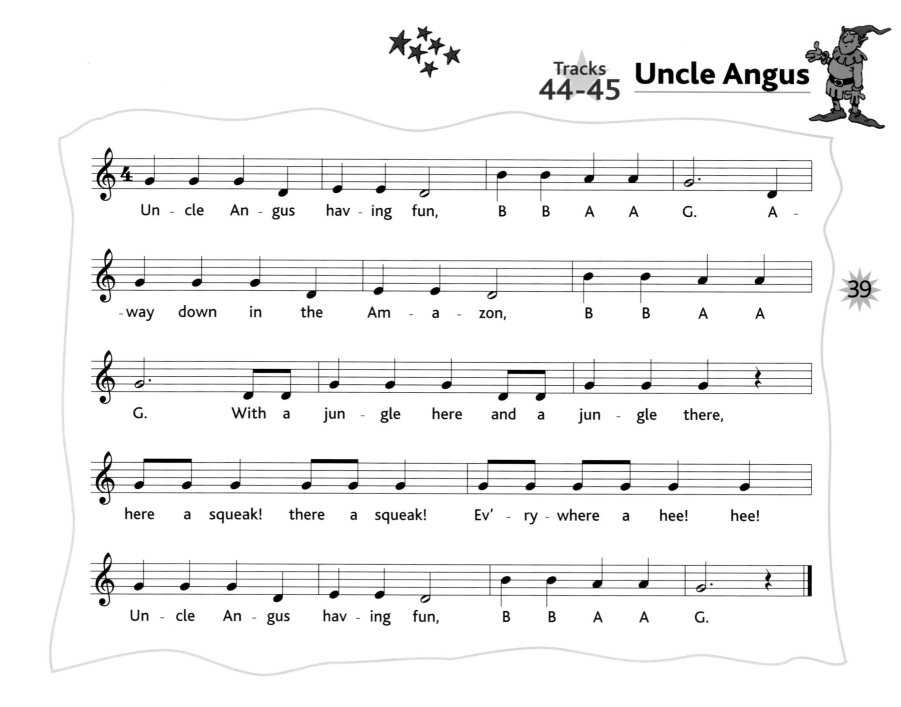

39

Answers to Puzzles

Copy Cat page 19
G, A, B

Rhythm Puzzle page 25
The rhythms from the song are clapped in this order:

Secret Words page 31
The secret words are: BAD, AGE, EGG, DAD, DEAD, BADGE

Welcome to My Home Puzzle page 33
The password is: BAGGAGE

40

CD Track Listing

Page numbers in brackets.
Each tune has two tracks – the first is a
model recorder version; the second is the
backing track only.

1	Introduction (3)
2-3	Magic B (9)
4-5	Play with A (11)
6-7	Dance with Me (12)
8	Copy Cat (14)
9-10	G Is for Ghost (15)
11-12	Three Blind Mice (17)
13-14	Mary Had a Little Lamb (18)
15	Copy Cat (19)
16-17	E Is for Enchanted (20)
18-19	Enchanted E (21)
20	Forest Sounds (22)
21-22	Enchanted Forest (23)
23	Song of the Elves (24)
24-25	D Is for Dragon (26)
26-27	Tiger Lilies (27)
28-29	The Dragon's Lair (28)
30-31	Under Attack! (29)
32-33	Lullaby (30)
34-35	March to the Castle (32)
36-37	Clock Chimes (34)
38-39	Trumpet Fanfare (35)
40-41	Celebrate! (36)
42-43	Dancing Elves (37)
44-45	Uncle Angus (39)
46	Farewell from the Recorder Wizard!

Printed in Singapore